To order additional copies of this book, contact:
Xlibris
1-888-795-4274
www.Xlibris.com
Orders@Xlibris.com

ISBN: 978-1-9845-8863-0 (sc)
ISBN: 978-1-9845-8864-7 (hc)
ISBN: 978-1-9845-8862-3 (e)

Library of Congress Control Number: 2020913170

Print information available on the last page

Rev. date: 07/20/2020

My Epiphany

Bahador Ghahramani

In a grain of sand, imagine the expansive universe

Awareness of mystical intrigue

In light of sight, seek the preciousness of life

Amazement of universe as self and self as universe

To Shahla,

I wish to live until one breath before you, my love

To hold your hands to the very end

I will look into your eyes for the last time

Then will wait for you at the pearly gate beyond

ACKNOWLEDGMENTS

The author acknowledges his family, friends, and colleagues for their contributions, talents, and time to support preparation and publications of *My Epiphany*. Furthermore, he extends his special and sincere gratitude to

- Professor David McAleavey, George Washington University, for reviewing, commenting, and publishing recommendations.
- Professor Fleur Tehrani, California State University Fullerton, for reviewing, commenting, formatting suggestions, and publishing guidance.
- Professor Virginia (Ginny) Greiman, Harvard University, for reviewing, commenting, and publishing references.
- Director Kent Kettell, colleague, for reviewing, editing, and designing the cover.
- Debra Sanders, colleague, for reviewing, commenting, and editing.

PREFACE

My Epiphany poems

- Are celestial messages revealed to the author in their original form and order with minor editions.
- Reference to "love" designates a mystical and conscious love, not erotic but selfless.

My Epiphany

I

Share with me my life's epiphany

My trials and mystical journey

Serenades of wisdoms revealed truly

My conscious thoughts and their hegemony

II

A fool praising the wise is futile

A fool degrading the wise is unconceivable

A wise recognizing a fool is common sense

The wise demeaning a fool is unforgivable

III

When I am dismayed, you are my shelter

I am darkened, you are my light

When I am doubted, you are my harbor

I am disconcerted, you are my strength

IV

I have witnessed war, famine, and injustice

At awe with the resiliency of human spirit

I have seen suffering, oppression, and abuse

Allured by humanity's will to overcome plight

V

In water, wind, earth, and fire

I perceive tranquility everywhere

In my soul, mind, conscious, and all conceivable

I am cognizant of divine cosmic love

VI

Nothing can bring back our bygone loves

Thoughtful moments of unforgettable happiness

Neither can remedy our lost tenderness

Treasured time imprinted on the chambers of our hearts

VII

Every step into mythology is a biopic to my spirit

One sway upward is an ascending plight

Every span of my wings is a soaring flight

One stride is a thrust toward heavenly stardust

VIII

Is life revealed by providence or evolution?

Is spirit incepted by heaven or nature?

It is all a matter of interpretation

I believe in divinity of spirit and serenity of life

IX

Life is not measured by age

Wealth, wisdom, or knowledge

Life is measured by the differences made

When one is willing, dedicated, and able

X

At times, I feel like a spirited bird, caged with broken wings

Yearning to break free from earthly constraints

At that time, I imagine my freedom by spreading my wings

Yet I have to wait until my soaring flight returns

XI

In a grain of sand, imagine the expansive universe

Awareness of mystical intrigue

In light of sight, seek the preciousness of life

Amazement of universe as self and self as universe

XII

I cannot promise you an everlasting peace

But will give you my unconditional love

I cannot shelter you from misfortunes of life

But will give you all the love I can have

XIII

There is no heavier burden than guilt

Forever tarnishing the spirit

There is no greater tragedy than a trust lost

Fore long wondering, "Why not?"

XIV

Wherever my journey takes me, I feel a part

Whoever I see, I am a part

Within my soul, I feel this celestial sentiment

Whether I am all that is or all is in my thought

XV

Perfection is possible by trials and errors

A diamond turns precious by frictions

Prosperity is not without disappointments

Adversity overcomes by challenges

XVI

I love the smell of salt and sand on the seashore

Beauty of magical sunrise and sunset in the skyline

I cherish the mosaic of seaweeds' foliage on the seaside

Besieged by rainbow of colors in the coastline

XVII

Life gives you the opportunity for happiness

No burdens that you can't overcome

Live this moment as tomorrow may never comes

No matter how your fortune surmises

XVIII

Sound of weeping rain and thunder

Brings memories of my childhood prayer

Solemn providence, help me savor

Bygone joyful past and hopeful future

XIX

Eternity is an infinite state of exploration

Where imagination is boundless

Everlasting grandeur of universal design

Where love of humanity is priceless

XX

No child is to be a failure

No love is to be unreachable

No dream is to be impossible

No miracle is to be unbelievable

XXI

If love drives out hate

Then forgiveness surpasses vengeance

If hate is a burden to contemplate

Then love is infallible and hate is indefensible

XXII

In the book of life, your honesty is the first of chapters

Your passion to inspire and motivate is an example

In all your actions, you are to become wiser by strides

Your will thrusts you to the pinnacle of excellence

XXIII

We are torn between our earthly and spiritual transformation

From the dawn of creation, this has been our epic discovery

Wisdom of duality driving our mortal and immortal states

Forever this drama will shape our tranquility

XXIV

Deep within us dwells an awesome power realized

Strength that energizes us when propelled

Drawing from our power is knowledge gained

Summoning life's trials are conceived

XXV

I seek providence in all creeds governing my odyssey

    Churches, synagogues, mosques, and temples are analogous

I am at awe with believers of all faiths shaping humanity

    Charity of good thoughts, good words, and good deeds

XXVI

Suppose you ask two spiritual questions

    "What is the secret of life?" Or "Why are we born, and

why do we die?"

Simply refer to the depth of your cognitive conscious

    Where life's answers reside

XXVII

If ideals are not reached, still hope

    They are dreams of us that stay awake

If ideals are the lasting notions to recognize

    They are our guiding lights through life

XXVIII

From the dawn of humanity, it is asked

Is there a supreme providence creator of all?

For me, this question is already answered

I believe in the miracle of life large and small

XXIX

Greatness is exoneration of critical rationale

Fallacy of collective revealing thoughts

Grandeur of accumulated knowledge

Free from sensual temptations

XXX

No reason to carry on adversities of yesterdays

Pains of broken promises

Never reminisce on the betrayal of friends

Ponder on the prosperities of tomorrows

XXXI

I am aware of four virtues to abide:

   Temperance, wisdom, justice, and fortitude

I have followed them throughout my life

   Though I may never measure up to their platitude

XXXII

Suppose you ask, "Is there a spiritual awareness?"

   "Are there cosmic intelligences?"

Searching through your cognitive conscious

   Answers are sparked within imprints of your visions

XXXIII

There are three secrets to life's success:

   First, know yourself truly

Two, listen to your heart and follow your dreams

   Finally, live passionately

XXXIV

Sights can only see surroundings

Immaculate vision perceives intelligences

Seek intelligent foresight to spark purity of awareness

Imagination to conceive imminent insights

XXXV

Since providence conceived in you cosmic thoughts

Then foresight is transcended in you

Since you inherited universal conscious

Then you are a totality of universe and universe is a

totality of you

XXXVI

I often think of events forming my life

My hopes and dreams affecting my odyssey

I try to reason all in any form or shape

My life revolves around calamity and serenity

XXXVII

I am in peace with dualities surrounding me

    Past and present, or nights and days

I am also in harmony with dualities within me

    Passion and reason, or mind and conscious

XXXVIII

Hoping is a driver of the soul

    Breaking away from consciousness of unreal to real

Heeding reality to face subliminal

    Becoming aware of known to prevail

XXXIX

I have been asked, "When was life incepted?"

    Whether it began when the universe evolved?

It is a quandary that is agelessly pondered

    Where answers are transpired from our celestial mind

XL

Be free from shackles of personal vendettas

Open your heart to heavenly thoughts

Behold to life's enchanted treasures

Overcome profane beliefs and rejoice forever longs

XLI

A true friend is worth more than gold

Is irreplaceable, indispensable, and solid

A friend's affection is always justified

Is without expectations and never compromised

XLII

If dreams are revelations of our conscious

Then every dream emanates from our subconscious

If dreams are projections of our embedded desires

Then they are inherent desires without reflections

XLIII

Often I feel burdens upon my feeble life

Testing my inner convictions without any hope

Others see in me no recourse to overcome

Then I prevail by reaching my pinnacle purpose

XLIV

Our morality is not dependent on earthly treasures

But our willingness to help those who need care

Our spirituality is the only way to reach utopian mysticisms

By the ultimate test of humanity for reverence

XLV

You are conceived as an infant of humanity

With all its trappings and distinctions

You are revealed in the name of spirituality

With all its hopes and dreams

XLVI

Childhood impressions become youthful reality

Youthful reality becomes aged creativity

Creativity becomes thoughtful intensity

Thoughtful intensity becomes renewed capability

XLVII

Let flame of love burn in my heart

A flame fevering essence of my plight

Let my passion emanate as a bright light

A glow leading me through my mystical flight

XLVIII

Everyone is a new novel full of wonders

Each life is a story of tragedies and triumphs

Everlasting legacy of trials and turbulences

Eternal impression of spiritual intrigues

XLIX

I fear neither death nor unknowns

    Not attached to worldly fortunes

I have no dread of living my ways

    No regrets of loving you times after times

L

Forever sing joy of furious love

    Songs of romance and heart's triumphs

Fear no despair and remorse

    Selfless hope of brighter tomorrows

LI

Eternity is beyond time and space

    Where our cosmic thought beholds

Ecstasy is the true love of life

    Where allure of life never fades

LII

My love of humanity flows with vitality

It is the essence of my immortality

My passion is believing in spirituality

It is invaluable beyond reality

LIII

I cry for the inhumanity to others and feel their agony

For those who are harmed and never heard

I pain for the oppressed in captivity

For lives broken and dreams abandoned

LIV

Hope is a state of the heart, not mind

Soothing the psychic when intrigued

Hope keeps our compass unobscured

Silently inspiring us enthused

LV

As you appear, surrounding glows

My heart races and day brightens

As you near, angels serenade heavenly songs

My happiness prolongs

LVI

Whoever my path crosses is a gift to remember

An occasion imprinted in my everlasting memory

Wherever I explore is a canvas to wonder

An eternal treasure resonating through my ecstasy

LVII

We long for an intellectual consciousness

Although it may not be palatable

We hear the inner voice of our ethics

Always clear and recognizable

LVIII

Many lonely paths traveled to seek knowledge

Seen many lands near and far distance

Mastered my destiny and chartered my life

Sought wisdom and gained ultimate exuberance

LIX

Whichever unknown destination traveled

I am fascinated by love of others

Wherever I have journeyed

I am overwhelmed by strangers' goodness

LX

If our freedom of expression is taken away

We will be silenced and not heard

If we are without free will and liberty

We will be mindless herds subjugated

LXI

Hear call of nature's wild

    As it resonates through your mind

Heed to beauty of wildernesses' calls summoned

    Allow your senses to feast as you are surmised

LXII

Often heartaches may overwhelm your life

    Sorrows may circumvent your dreams

Otherwise, your efforts may seem futile

    Seek inner strength to mend your pains

LXIII

In my wondrous fascination

    I am journeying beyond imagination

In a state of celestial transformation

    I am risen to a divine creation

LXIV

Life is a spinning wheel turning

Spinning around and around

Let go of your unhappy feeling

Sorrow no more, leave them behind

LXV

If impression is reality

Then reality is the ultimate believability

If believability encompasses conscionability

Then conscionability is the decisive judgementality

LXVI

You may ask, "What if I was born a more desirable person?"

Richer, wiser, younger, and with better features

Your answer is embedded within your conscious unseen

Revealed in you are all of the desired attributes

LXVII

Four fundamental forces are governing our physical universe

They are centrally weaving our surrounding space

For me, two other evolving powers are in existence

They are conscious thought and spiritual cognizance

LXVIII

Wherever I see flight of migrant birds

I wish to soar with them higher and free

Whenever I hear adventures of wandering travelers

I yearn to be with them farther and free

LXIX

Was asked "What is the secret of intelligence?"

Answered, "Perceiving all as miracles to experience!"

Was asked, "What would this experience enable me?"

Answered, "To know yourself as you truly are!"

LXX

Often, I hear subliminal words and feel their tones

But cannot understand the meaning of their message

Other times, I am at odds with the message as it resonates

Bewildered by what I hear but cannot refute

LXXI

I have no regrets of what I have done

I regret all that I could but have not done

If I am to live a hundred years to come

I will love life 'til the end of time

LXXII

No matter what age or gender

There is an insatiable lure to forever wonder

Neither days nor nights resolve our sadness or cheer

Thinker to thought that life is to forever wander

LXXIII

Life is like grains of sand in an hour glass

Full of promises as it begins

Leave your sorrows behind that they too will pass

Forewarned that your end will soon arrives

LXXIV

Honesty leads us through our obstacles

It is a guide to choose right over wrong

Having it right when time comes

Is to choose right forever long

LXXV

Let us feel the softness of raindrops

Listening to the sound of thunders

Let me shelter you through storms

Leaving behind turbulent thoughts

LXXVI

Go as far as your imagination leads

Then imagine farther

Give love to as many as your heart desires

Then love further

LXXVII

Let passion shape our lives forever

Let it be the companion of our inner power

Let hope dictate our lives hereafter

Let it diminish our differences ever after

LXXVIII

Imagine soaring on wings of time and space infinites

Anxiously exploring life's hidden treasures

Impressions of love to become aware beyond all bounds

Astonished by a world full of adventures

LXXIX

Look into an hourglass unfolding

      As its grains of sand pouring softly

Love life as today is yours lasting

      As days of life passing like sand slowly

LXXX

My secret rose garden is my treasured refuge

      Each rose is unique to behold and love

Mystery is in their beauty, fragrance, and allure

      Ecstatic whenever I am close to a blooming rose

LXXXI

What we are hoping for is what we are dreaming for

      Understanding of what we are striving for

What hope is meant is what we are living for

      Ultimate desire we are achieving for

LXXXII

Where are you, my love, now that you are gone?

I searched for you, but to no avail

Wherever I turn, I see your image

I will always love you above all

LXXXIII

Life's challenges are rebounds to our spirits

When facing agitations and adversities

Love and hate are inherent parts of our natures

When feeling in love, our despair subsides

LXXXIV

If you feel down, listen to your conviction within

You hear the divine melody of inspiration

If you feel misplaced and uncertain

Your strength rests on your determination

LXXXV

Memories are personification of mind

       Highlighting all that is transpiring but long passed

Marveling life's miracles as it is resonated

       Holding to all that is precious and forever inspired

LXXXVI

Nurture your river of passion and fly on wings of dreams

       Be cognizant of your inner divine voice

Never mind your earthly impulses

       Become one with mysticism of your conscious

LXXXVII

What is life without love?

       Or love without hope

What is hope without intelligence?

       Or intelligence without knowledge

LXXXVIII

A true friend is as invaluable as can be

Never wavering your intentions

An honorable enemy is preferred to a naive mate

Nothing replaces a friend who has no expectations

LXXXIX

No matter how the sun rises or sets

Whether birds soar over mountains

Not knowing all is not as regrettable as

Waiting for a true love as life subsides

XC

Anticipation is a sanctuary from suspension

When one door is closed, persevere, others open

Anticipation excites our hearts for an expectation

Wait, weary days turn to a hopeful premonition

XCI

I am what I am, believing in what I believe

My own rudder, sailing through life's mystical ecstasy

I am trailing toward a cosmic intelligence

My own path to infallibility

XCII

Sanctity of all lives is beyond honor

No matter in what shape, form, and gender

Sacredness of one life is as another

No reproach if conceived by a divine power

XCIII

Life without love is devoid of fulfillment

Love without compassion is a futile pursuit

Live life knowing that all will circumvent

Leave sorrows, soar with love in your flight

XCIV

Through the window of my soul, I see eternal fascination

Grandeur of all that is in my perception

Tapestry of never-ending constellation

Greatness of life as a precious creation

XCV

Do not walk behind or in front of me

Walk with me and keep me company

Do share your hopes and dreams with me

Welcome me through life's ecstasy

XCVI

I was asked "Which one would you choose—wealth or

knowledge?"

Answered, "I choose knowledge"

I was asked "Why knowledge?"

Answered, "Without knowledge, wealth is futile"

XCVII

If we hope for a perfect world, we will not succeed

World is not perfectly created

If we wish for a perfect life, we will be disappointed

Willing to make a difference, we will succeed

XCVIII

Strive to be as best as you can

Make right choices and follow a virtuous path

Surpass your life's expectations and follow your passion

Master your will and fulfill your faith

XCIX

We all depart from life's mortal journey

Leaving behind our fames and fortunes

What matters is our goodwill passed away

Legacy of life's unconditional love toward others

C

Maturity is wisdom gained from experience

Leaving what you can't achieve for later

Making friends no matter your difference

Loving all those you encounter

CI

I asked a traveler, "Where are you heading?"

He answered, "Where my love resides"

I envied the traveler for his forthcoming

He had found his fountain of happiness

CII

Our lives begin when we start being righteous

End when we are silent to injustices

Or fulfilled when we are generous

Enriched when we are courageous

CIII

Faith is an everlasting glow

    Serenity of believing in tomorrow

Feeling a desire to outreach the hollow

    Setting a righteous course to follow

CIV

Heed to wisdom of the aged

    Hear to the advice of those you caressed

Hallowed is guidance of ones you cared

    Hope to reach your dreams as you perceived

CV

Lord, I ask for no wealth and comfort

    No treasures and worldly ransoms

Lead me to an eternal love and inspiring thought

    No hope to live without either reasons

CVI

Though searching for enlightenment near and far

I am unable to confess being lost forever

Tirelessly probing for a utopia to surrender

I am destined to timelessly wonder

CVII

Glue that holds relations is trust

If trust is broken, friendship will never last

Gems are rough like trust until finally turned radiant

If their ecstatics are right, they turn to star bright

CVIII

Sunrises softly engulfing fluffy mists

Splendor of winter is weathering streams

Surfs are caressing shallow marshes

Silence of dawn is broken by sandpipers' calls

CIX

My divine love is spiritually omnipresent

Is revealing as sanctity of conscious thought

Mystical and eternally omnipotent

Illuminating from chambers of my heart

CX

Taking adversities personally, we suffer consequently

Their ripple effects will be concurrently

Time heals when life throws anguish unexpectedly

Taking what comes our way prudently

CXI

Everyone is a new chapter in our book of memories

A novel full of intrigues and glories

Every encounter is one of our legacies

An unabated chain bonding our humanities

CXII

Mother's love is deeper than the vastest oceans

Warmer than sunshine bright

Mightier than the grandest summits

Welcoming wholeheartedly and is permanent

CXIII

Life is defined by your choices

Remembered by your failures and achievements

Love yourself as you never loved others

Resolute your strength and overcome failures

CXIV

Consciousness is a warning light in darkness of indecision

Guiding us toward our desire to take action

If not listened, it condemns us as a guilty villain

Guilt is a judge of ill decisions dwelling within

CXV

Beyond cognizance, revealed a universal spirit

A canvas of insights surpassed

Beyond awareness, searched for a celestial thought

A discovery of mysteries sustained

CXVI

Take me away on the wings of imagination

To a peaceful haven free from mortal constraints

Take my soul to where time has no dimension

To where there are no feeble temptations

CXVII

I hear nightingales calling

Singing to the moon as they are dancing

I envy their love of life while reciting

Serenading love as they are rejoicing

CXVIII

Shrouded in life's mystery, each vision is a miracle

Every sound is a musical wonder

Surprises abound, no matter where

Endless belief in a universal splendor

CXIX

Can there be wisdom without freedom of thought?

I believe not!

Confinement of ideas are a detriment to human edict

I live for liberty of will without any constraint

CXX

Change is in time, you must have faith

Your soul is touched by angels' calls, forever abound

Charge ahead, you are the essence of a universal gift

Your life has a purpose to behold

CXXI

I welcome life's unknowns facing me

Surprising me at every juncture

I am ready for whatever is confronting me

Sunrise to sunset, I am exuberantly alive

CXXII

What is sanctity of life without a purpose to strive for?

A reason to live and reach shining ideals

Willing to overcome obstacles and feeling triumphant for

A desire to make a difference against all odds

CXXIII

I am a soothsayer foreseeing your fortunes

Welcoming you to my world of spirituality

I am foreseeing enlightenment to your happiness

Wishing you a fulfilling life eternally

CXXIV

My Ahura is omnipresent in darkness and lightness

In cosmic thoughts and universal awareness

My Ahura is omnipotent in manners and forms

Is omniscient in finites and infinites

CXXV

Since dawn of time, sages have pondered

What is the meaning of life?

So far as I know, the answer for me is revealed

What my life is to pursue cognizance and eternal love

CXXVI

Somewhere beyond imagination, magic resides

Where tranquility surpasses

Somehow I shall reach this refuge of enchantments

When, I do not know, will try to the end of times

CXXVII

I am a teacher, scholar, and entrepreneur

Traveler, philosopher, and soothsayer

I have pursued conscious thought everywhere

Through it all, "I am a true believer!"

CXXVIII

My love, never say never

No matter what is destined in our future

My love, never fill your heart with fear

No matter if we are near or far

CXXIX

Give me passion to be pious

Conviction to be righteous

Grant me foresight to be virtuous

Courage to follow my conscious

CXXX

I love the spring breeze awakening my senses

When flowers dance with swerving grasses

In harmony with blooming nature as it soothes my ways

When season's effulgence engulfs the wilderness

CXXXI

Lifelong pursuit of awareness, not understood

Searched for understanding in four corners of the world

Looked for revelation of consciousness to behold

Summoned in search of awareness, surrendered

CXXXII

Is it better to do right for the wrong reasons?

Or to do wrong for the right reasons?

I am unable to answer any of these questions

Only, I follow my conscious

CXXXIII

Life does not end on this earthly voyage

It shines forever as an eternal flame

Live life as an awesome miracle

It is as sacred as an amazing adventure

CXXXIV

I cannot ask for an eternal life

We all have to depart sooner or later

I only ask for a peaceful passage

Where I can be in serenity here and after

CXXXV

In depth of my thought, I know my cognitive limitations

Foreseeing no boundaries to my intrinsic innervations

I am fully accepting all challenges to my aspirations

Fearing none, reaching beyond all my expectations

CXXXVI

It is the poet, not the poem

    The singer, not the song

It is the dreamer, not the dream

    The explorer, not the exploring

CXXXVII

If your heart is to be filled with love, stay

    Share your love until eternity

If your heart is set to be free, fly away

    Seek wherever your love may wish to journey

CXXXVIII

Live life to the fullest, that all is only a mirage

    No one knows how tomorrow will surmise

Love life, that all is a fable

    Nothing is real, and all is a facade

CXXXIX

I love you because I believe in you

    I rave for you from the depth of my heart

I believe in you because I love you

    I cannot live without your thought

CXL

Let me hear singing of love ballads

    Gaze with me to the vastness of blue yonder

Let me dream of drowning in your eyes

    Give me your heart forever after

CXLI

There is a star in heaven shining upon each of us

    Sparkling in harmony with our heartbeats

Timely reminder of our lives' trials

    Seamless passage to our imprints

CXLII

Hear ballads of ancient heroes

      Everlasting stories of bygone triumphs

Honor recitals of their sagas

      Eternal songs of endless glories

CXLIII

I wish to live until one breath before you, my love

      To hold your hands to the very end

I will look into your eyes for the last time

      Then will wait for you at the pearly gate beyond

CXLIV

Trust me with your pains

      Welcome me into your heart

Tell me your sorrows

      Whether we are near or apart

CXLV

When spring arrives, nature awakens into a rainbow of colors

A burst of beauty as blossoms swerve and wind blows

When spring fades, a feeling of lost beauty rests

As I yearn to venture my canopy of spring blossoms

CXLVI

Unhappiness is not achieving what we can accomplish

Starting what we cannot carry through

Utopia is when our dreams are within reach

Seeking higher ideals to flourish

CXLVII

Winning is a strive to perform well

An ability to outgrow infinitesimal

Worth is not what you acquire or will

A willingness to achieve all

CXLVIII

Lack of affection resonates from our heartaches

Love of life prevents us from misfortunes

Love others as though tomorrow will never comes

Live life to the fullest as our love forever lasts

CXLIX

Adaptability is not a weakness and limitation

It is a form of assimilation and attribution

All problems may have more than one unique resolution

Indeed, seeking happiness is our only retribution

CL

Was asked, "What is caring?"

Answered, "Willing to do others right, not wrong"

Was asked, "What is right?"

Answered, "Following your conscious forever long"

CLI

Whether you are rich or poor, all will be succumbed

What matters is your goodness left behind

Without goodness, your fate is compromised

When the end comes, richness is only a state of your mind

CLII

Ah, I cherish memories of bygone days

Trials of childhood innocence

Affinity of youthful carefree plays

Twilight of unforgettable years of adolescence

CLIII

I am anxious to seek new paths to venture

Times to flourish and abundance

Is it wrong to hope for new horizons to explore?

Times of fruition as hope shows its relevance

CLIV

Eternally in debt to heroism of past patriots

Who have kept the faith and fought the fight

Everlasting gratitude to freedom fighters

Who have sacrificed all with undying spirit

CLV

When do we stop inhumanity to others?

My restless soul has no answers

What can I do to stop oppressions?

My life is in one with the oppressed, always

CLVI

If I could bet on the future

I bet on the magnificence of human spirit

If I could have a crystal ball to foresee the future

I seek a path to subliminal conscious thought

CLVII

Can I ever transcend to dimensionless havens?

Where my physical bounds are freed into spiritual blooms

Carefree from earthly shackles

Where my soul soars in peace without burdens

CLVIII

Adversity is a state of awareness in our lives

Without adversaries' trials, life is meaningless

As life's turbulences shadow our dreams

Worries subside by our hope's brightness

CLIX

I hear sound of bugles and beat of drums calling

I envision lightning of bayonets ricocheting

I am at awe with my comrades bravely charging

I honor our freedom fighters as they are marching

CLX

Let chambers of your heart burn in fury of love

Fire in your soul ignite passion in your life

Let this feverish flame lead you to a lasting peace

Forever rejoice your love without any penitence

CLXI

Intuition is emergence of a new insight

A burst of mythical visions

It pronounces reason to express a thought

A desire to reach knowns from unknowns

CLXII

There will never be another love

Like my love for you

There will never be anyone else

Like my passion for you

CLXIII

Whether perseverance is a substitute for talent

It is the best possible stride for it

Whether productivity is a substitute for contentment

It is the revelation of self-fulfillment

CLXIV

In the restlessness of my heart

I envision the reflection of your smiles

In the depth of my spirit

I hear hymns singing your praises

CLXV

Silkiness of blue sky gives me warmth

Solitude of forest gives me insight

Serenity of insight gives me strength

Serving humanity gives me all I have dreamt

CLXVI

I love walking on the seashores

       Listening to the seagulls hovering over the marshes

I am fascinated, gazing at the stardust shining through clouds

       Lonely stroll along the misty streams

CLXVII

Your love has resurrected me

       Inspired my affection into the future

You have given me meaning to my life

       Intrigued a dialogue for my existence

CLXVIII

Whatever you perceive, you can achieve

       Your perception encompasses your value

Whatever you wish, it can come true

       Your resolute is your divine resolve

CLXIX

Our lives are not measured by the number of breaths we take

But by actions that take our breaths away

Our destinies are not shaped by wishes beyond our drive

But by determination through our life's journey

CLXX

Enthusiasm is an inner drive resonating to others

A state of mind that radiates

Everlasting perception of profoundness

A desire to share life's fortunes with others

CLXXI

Somewhere over there, days are mild

Skyline is blue, meshing with white sand

Sunrise in horizon is emanating through cloud

Splendor of being in one with the wild

CLXXII

I shall return to your arms

Where my love rests

I shall return to your inviting smiles

Where my happiness resides

CLXXIII

The ones you love never abate

Their memories are eternally divine

They may leave, but their loves will endure

Toll of their loves never subside

CLXXIV

Have you ever wondered, "What is it all about?"

Tried to understand mysteries of universes within and

without

Here is my thought, follow your dream and listen to your heart

Then reach to your spiritual awareness and reflect

CLXXV

My desire to explore is leading me to unbeaten paths

Every step is guiding me as wondering subsides

My eagerness is entrusting me into unknowns

Every uncertainty is treasured without rhymes and reasons

CLXXVI

When your days turn to bad

Hope for better days

When you try but can't succeed

Heed for future victories

CLXXVII

What is there that calls me from distances?

Messages from subliminal unknowns

What is there that hounds my soul to restlessness?

Murky yearning to epic ventures

CLXXVIII

Sages say beauty is not a reflection outside

But a spark of wisdom shining inside

Seek wisdom as your anchor to stride

Behold to your rudder and forever shine

CLXXIX

Infallible is conscious thought

Where it inherits knowledge ever known

Indestructible is human spirit

Where it animates from inner perception

CLXXX

If we were angels, no need for governesses

No need for laws and divine scriptures

If spiritual awareness could govern our earthly desires

No legacy of inhumanity to others

CLXXXI

When spring blooms, I am allured by my roses

When nurtured, they trigger my senses

Without true love of life, my garden is without its roses

Wondering not, life is as colorful as my canopy of roses

CLXXXII

Bright moon graces the heavens

Silence is broken by calls of wilderness

Brisk wind hovers over hazy meadows

Symphony of whispering breeze soothes my senses

CLXXXIII

We differ in our ability to perform

Different in our "will to conform"

We see reality as a judge of human mechanism

Demand freedom and devoid unknown despotism

CLXXXIV

I shall return to sanctity of where I was born

    Where the surrounding is full of memories

I shall return to the love I have known

    Where my true happiness resides

CLXXXV

Art's mystery is in its design, creation, and color

    Is in redemption of beauty and hidden treasure

Artist's revelation is from spirit to observer

    Is in imagination resonating through its nature

CLXXXVI

Passion, persuasion, and patience

    Turns a dream into its actuality

Presents meaning where there is none

    Takes an impression from uncertainty to its certainty

CLXXXVII

Farewell, our journey may never cross again

Forever, your memory is transcended in my heart

Fever you left in my soul is never forgotten

Feeling grateful for sharing your thought

CLXXXVIII

Honor your passion to cultivate and create

Let imagination pilot your desires

Harvest gratefully fruits of your fortune

Let faith gracefully show your ways

CLXXXIX

It may be disheartening to try and fail

It is unacceptable not to try at all

It is not the game, but how to reach the goal

It is the effort, not outcome of the trial

CXC

If it is love or hate, I choose love

Hate is too heavy a burden to carry

If it is hope or despair, I choose hope

Hope is my sanctuary to reach spirituality

CXCI

For long, I have pursued knowledge, wisdom, and tranquility

Traveled near and far through my ecstasy

Forever, I have helped, served, and loved humanity

To the fullest, I lived and left my legacy

CXCII

Within the crowd, I feel lonely for your arms

Where I can share with you my thoughts

With you, I feel no restlessness

Where I can serenade to you my love vows

CXCIII

I love you for what you truly are

My feeling is formidable more than imaginable

I cannot measure our love; it is impossible

My love transcends our hearts into a flaming fire

CXCIV

Be kind to the aged as they reflect

Their wisdom of years past

Behold that your turn will follow next

Tinker to the thought that youth will never last

CXCV

Life is a bridge from present known to future unknown

A manifestation of our hopes and dreams

Let our hearts' imprints echo what we have been

Assimilation of our desire to achieve higher consciousness

CXCVI

In the midst of fire and fury, see your inner light

Shining upon and leading you to Shangri-La

In depth of darkness and despair, ascend beyond your plight

Summoning your strength to refuge in the ultimate utopia

CXCVII

My love for you has neither beginning nor ending

You are the soul and essence of my conscious

My love knows no sanctuary from hiding

Your love is the wind beneath my wings

CXCVIII

Do not count the times you spend wondering

Clearest way to your resolve is by self-reflection

Desire inner beauty as life is worth living

Come along with me and seek redemption

CXCIX

If eyes are mirrors of the soul

Then love is a mirror of the heart

If consciousness is a mirror of all

Then deed is a mirror of want

CC

No matter who you are and what you believe

You will have a special place in my heart

Never regret our togetherness through life

You have touched my conscious and risen my spirit

CCI

Listen to whisper of sonatas imprinted on your heart

Beats of your inner symphony

Listen to the depth of your thought

Breaking stillness of silence through your odyssey

CCII

Hope is an everlasting heart's shadow

Dividing today's reality from unreal tomorrow

Hope of future is all we need to know

Desire to set the right course to follow

CCIII

It is not what you believed

What you achieved

It is not what you learned

Whether you made a difference

CCIV

No delusion of reaching eternal happiness

No matter what my heart desires

Never thriving on self-gratifications

Not carrying bitterness is my happiness

CCV

Our love is an affinity that links humanity together

A universal synthesis that will last forever

Our passion is serene with lasting fever

An unconditional splendor without waiver

CCVI

Success shows us the achievement side of our lives

Adversity leads us to understand our nature

Solitude gives us value and strengthens our resolves

Ask for virtue, it is our lasting treasure

CCVII

The relativity theory reveals the gravitational state of infinite

universe

It is within the realm of cosmological and astrophysical

The singularity theory reveals the space-time finite universe

I surmise that all is to wonder and wonder is to all

CCVIII

When I am hopeless, you are my shelter

When shadows are overwhelming, you are my light

When I am lost, you are my harbor

When I am frail, you are my might

CCIX

Forever, I have carried fever of your love too long

Fiery, in solitude of my broken heart

For long, I am lost without your thought, come along

Fury, longing for the shadow of your smile, I am lost

CCX

It is not what you believed or achieved

Nor knowledge you learned or practiced

It is not worldly possessions you gathered

None are as worthy as the love you gained

CCXI

Emanates from you are three of life's marvels

Finite body, divine spirit, and eternal consciousness

Eternal consciousness is your soul's insights

Forever, it is a legacy intrinsic into your awareness

CCXII

In times of desolation

Reach to the depth of your soul for resolution

In times of fulfillment, find absolution

Regardless of each, soar beyond imagination

CCXIII

Resolute to follow your dreams

Never shelter behind your fears

Regardless of what destiny holds

Never strive to be less than success

CCXIV

In the thunder, fire, and fury of my soul

I console to comfort of your arms

In the turmoil of my never-ending wonderous subliminal

I serenade you the fever of my subconscious

CCXV

My love for you has no boundaries and constraints

It knows no laws and seeks no rewards

My love for you is authentic and never ends

It is the glue bonding us forever lasts

CCXVI

I love you not because of what I gain in return

I love you because I have no other expectation

I love you till the dawn of creation

I love you whether you are healthy or in pain

CCXVII

I am of fire, water, earth, and time

I am of my soul, mind, thoughts, and desires

I am no more or less than what I am destined to be

I am of a living and breathing intricate universes

CCXVIII

My love for you is no less than vastness of universe

My love, I hold you tight because you are all mine

My love for you is above all that could be imaginable

My love, loving you is a state of tranquility and peace

CCXIX

I have no illusion to ever reaching ultimate perfection

It is not within my reach and aspiration

It is prevalent if I pursue spiritual perfection

I achieve excellence and carry mystical affection

CCXX

Now that my epiphany is shared

My wisdoms will be with you to the very end

Never compromise the wisdoms learned

May your life be as bright as you envisioned